Ever-Changing:

A Super Hero Manual Book

by

Daniel K. Arnold

Ever-Changing: A Super Hero Manual Book: Table of Contents

<u>Ever-Changing:</u>

<u>A Super Hero Manual Book</u>

Chapter 1: Introduction

I am a Super Hero. Not every day seems epic. Regardless, I seek to live my days for God.

A Super Hero is a person who lives supernaturally for Jesus, despite the realities of a disability. Super Heroes have the power to change the world. Some days feel phenomenal, some days are ordinary, and some days substandard. However, coping by the power of God, to be the best one can be, is epic.

Isaiah 40:30-31

"Even youths grow tired and weary, and young men stumble and fall; but those who hope in the LORD will

renew their strength. They will soar
on wings like eagles; they will run
and not grow weary, they will walk
and not be faint."

Ever-Changing:

A Super Hero Manual Book

Chapter 2: Mister Energy Plus

In **The Super Hero Manual**, Mister Energy Plus was seen on the cover. The explanation of the cover was segmented. Chapter 2 and Chapter 3 serve to flesh out the persona of Mister Energy Plus and his extra persona, "Black Bird Ops." The purpose of these two chapters is to case study a specific Super Hero type (mental disability coupled with spirituality) and demonstrate his/her capacity to glorify God.

Case Study:

Mister Energy Plus fits the archetype of the modern Type 2 Bipolar Disorder. He has moments of excessive energy as well as diminished energy. His rocket feet show his predicament of not being able to contain his momentum on his own. The blue bands encompassing his body demonstrate that he is functioning under a containment system. His belt shows that he is positively charged. His battery backpack contains two negative charged symbols showing that the Lithium charge balances out his excessive positive charge. The sun symbolizes his potential for pride and the Bible is held out in front of the sun to help him focus and calibrate with what's important. Theory is without these coping mechanisms, Mister Energy Plus, aka Daniel K. Arnold, would fly to the sun and burn up.

Theory:

Mister Energy Plus is coping, but has not always been. Many times he's glorified God with writing and leading Bible Study, but at other times he has spun out of control. He is far from perfect, but still manages to live an exciting life. He would not have it any other way.

Conclusion:

Take one day at a time. Be who you are meant to be. Cope with God's help and the resources God has put on this earth. "On hearing this, Jesus said, "It is not the healthy who need a doctor, but the sick. But go and learn what this means: 'I desire mercy, not sacrifice.' For I have not come to call the righteous, but sinners (Mark 2:17)."

Ever-Changing:

A Super Hero Manual Book

Chapter 3: Black Bird Ops

Black Bird Ops is a fantasy, yet real persona. Under this guise, Mister Energy Plus feels more significant and at the same time is more on edge. He becomes more aware of every sound and stimuli around him.

With a black mask on, he hides in the shadows and works to fight crime in his own way. Still wearing the lithium backpack, every bit of his uniform is stained in black for cover-up.

He holds a smaller Bible than before, with a cross on the center and acts rather seriously. He carries a pair of noids on either side of his shoulders and Abilify implants around his legs with the term ~~Ability~~ to represent the debilitation of the medication Abilify.

Schizoaffective is the world's stigma for Black Bird Ops.

Reality:

Sometimes Mister Energy Plus arises. Sometimes Black Bird Ops arises.

Is this a reality any Super Hero can face? David said in the Psalms, "With my God I can scale a wall (2 Samuel 22:30)."

Conclusion:

It's hard to face myself sometimes. This is an aspect of who I can be. I must rely on God to pick me up and salvage what's left of me. I need not hide behind a mask, but I cannot reveal everything to the world.

This is my predicament. This is my life. I've burned many bridges, but my real friends have stuck by me. It has been said that I am misunderstood.

As we do not have to live with sin, we do not have to live with our present condition. By faith, we can be ever changing from glory to glory. Even as our bodies decay, our minds can renew. Black Bird Ops, you do not have to stay.

"Do not conform to the pattern of this world, but be transformed by the renewing of your mind. Then you will be able to test and approve what God's will is--his good, pleasing and perfect will (Romans 12:2)."

I am unique. I am one-of-a-kind. My body is not perfect. Once again, I quote my Mom: "God made you and God made no junk."

<u>Ever-Changing:</u>

<u>A Super Hero Manual Book</u>

Chapter 4: New Day

I like when the sun comes out after a storm. "As far as the east is from the west, so far has he removed our transgressions from us
(Psalms 103:12)."

Yesterday can be truly over.

And when we begin a new moment, what do we think about?

It is certainly a great time to tune into the voice of God—a tune never regretted.

When God speaks those quiet unctions, man is changed, encouraged, transformed by the power of the Holy Ghost. I have had some God experiences that are out of this world.

"We walk by faith not by sight (2 Corinthians 5:7)."

"What do you want God to do for you?" (I heard a pastor say.)

I say dwell with me. Empower me to live a holy life. Put the right people around me. Bless my comings and my goings. Anything is possible with God. Do you really believe that?

Experience the anointing of the Lord God today!

"But the Comforter, which is the Holy Ghost, whom the Father will send in my name, He will teach you all things and bring all things to your remembrance—whatsoever I have said unto you (John 14:26)."

Do you know Jesus Lord supernaturally?

Has God spoken to you and blessed you with the gifts of the Holy Spirit?

He is real.

Pursue Him and He will give you understanding.

<u>Ever-Changing:</u>

<u>A Super Hero Manual Book</u>

Chapter 5: Deeper

I am not always sure of what to say or what to do. At moments like this, I tune into the voice of God.

I seek out confirmation of this voice and know that He will "never leave" me "nor forsake" me. He will speak and oh so clearly. He is ever-present and all-knowing. He truly cares.

Rest.

Let Him have control.

Let all fear subside.

Jesus is Lord!

The Super Hero and anyone can enter into bliss in the Lord. Dwelling with God is powerful as all distractions subside. The playing field is equalized as we sit and dine with a holy God who has torn away the separating veil that blocked communication.

Weaknesses become testimonies to draw in the broken.

Strengths are put in God's hands for His glory—"for every good and perfect gift comes from the Father of Lights (James 1:17)."

This is the season of joy and jubilee. This is the time believers come together in one accord.

We come to praise.

We come to rest in Him.

We come to hear God's voice, corporately as well as personally! Our experience is not always perfect; for we have imperfect senses.

One day we will have new bodies in true bliss. Until then, "Let everything that has breath praise the Lord (Psalms 150:7)!"

This is our season of breakthrough.

<u>Ever-Changing:</u>

<u>A Super Hero Manual Book</u>

Chapter 6: "Just Visiting"

The sorrows we encounter in life will not last. They are temporal. One man loses his child, another his leg. We are to "mourn with those who mourn."

In the same light, we should be happy with those who are happy. There is "a time for every purpose under Heaven (Ecclesiastes 3:1)."

This chapter is entitled, "Just Visiting" in reference to suffering. Our home is not on earth, but in Heaven.

Picture the game "Monopoly." Some passed through on the narrow portion of the game square and were "Just Visiting."

Others were actually stuck in jail.

Let us live our lives with an eternal perspective. Let us have an after-life to be looking forwards to. Let our sorrows be in a period of "Just Visiting."

We can learn something from suffering and picture how much Jesus had to pay that we might have eternal life.

It's time to be thankful for our future, grateful that we have this life to live, and thankful that God's changing our hearts for the better.

Next time you play Monopoly, remember that the narrow path is "Just Visiting" sorrow—great things are in store!

Ever-Changing:

A Super Hero Manual Book

Chapter 7: Lull Period

Not every day is meant to be exciting for the Super Hero.

"There is a time and purpose for every season under Heaven (Ecclesiastes 3:1)."

Some moments are for rest.

Some moments are for work.

Some moments are for spiritual recharging.

Recharging does not equate with feeling energetic, but rather balanced.

Like a rollercoaster, an abundance of feel good energy, does not equate with actual energy. The mind can be deceitful. True rest comes to those who spend time communing with God.

How much rest time is necessary is up to the individual hero and his/her Higher Power. Deposits made in the bank of rest with God benefit the hero, but balance is necessary there too.

Sabbath day comes once a week as God rested after six days. Balance is crucial to fulfill responsibilities. Nonetheless, it is a must for the hero to communicate with the God of Universe daily.
Focus is spent at this time. Energy is allocated to revere God and hear from him.

Even music takes time for rest periods. Everyone needs recovery time with God and the Super Hero is no exception.

Ever-Changing:

A Super Hero Manual Book

Chapter 8: Communication

We are on a commission from God.
As a unified Body of Christ,
"we are sent."

Although communication with God can involve the corporate Body, I believe it is most intimate on an individual basis. We, the Spirit-filled believers can tap into a realm of communication that is real, unique, clear, wonderful, and best of all, close to God. For the Godhead has entered our very beings.

Consultation with God can become direct in nature.

Nothing else is quite as genuine as hearing from the God within.

Namaste.

I greet the God in you because we are of the same spirit.

I am not referring to idolatry using the term "god", but the God who makes His home inside all true believers.

I am not here to please, but to be an agent of liberty. I am not the solution, but I know who holds it. Rest in the Lord. Be filled. Hold onto the promises of God.

Waahaaha…

Be the person God created you to be.

Do not shy away from being culturally relevant! We are to be "in the world but not of it."

Let "A Whole New World" in this same world captivate you.

This is the world of change. This is the world of being filled. "Delight yourself in the law of the Lord and He shall give you the desires of your heart." (Psalm 37:4) "What do you wish for Aladdin?"

God is no genie. He is actually all-powerful, but He will grant you new life and the desires of your heart if you seek Him with pure motive.

Live the dream life.

Live the free life.

Prosperity is connected with being prosperous. Blessings follow you where you go.

Why?

The Lord lavishes blessings on His children.

"But the Comforter, which is the Holy Ghost, whom the Father will send in my name. He will teach you all things and bring all things to your remembrance—whatsoever I have spoken unto you (John 14:26)."

All things means we will not have lack!

All things means that God is our final authority for wisdom and not mere man.

All things means certain breakthrough.

So "break on through to the other side. Break on through to the other side (Break On Through (To Other Side, The Doors)."

Ask God to open up the line of communication with you today!

<u>Ever-Changing:</u>

<u>A Super Hero Manual Book</u>

Chapter 9: What Do You Want?

Breakthrough happens when Christ's followers open their mouths and ask God for it. "Ye have not because ye ask not (James 4:2)," is not just a saying. It's a promise.

"What do you want out of life?" Christ followers. You took the time to obey God. Now look forwards!

"Delight yourself in the law of the Lord and He will give you the desires of your heart (Psalm 37:4)."

I like the classic song "Jesus On the Mainline." "Just call him up and tell Him what you want (Silvestri)."

What do you want out of life?

Since "all things are possible with God (Matthew 19:26)," it is time to stop settling for consolation. No, we are to "run as to get the prize (1 Corinthians 19:24)."

Case Study #1:

I walked down the street led by the Spirit. I asked for God's lead. When I became frustrated after walking far, I uttered, "God if you are truly leading this, let me run into someone I know."

Within minutes, I ran into a believer's house. "Ask, and it shall be given you; seek, and ye shall find; knock, and it shall be opened unto you (Matthew 7:7)."

Case Study #2:

My friend and I walked down M.A.C. Avenue to evangelize. We were led by the Spirit. Eventually, I said, "If we are really going to infiltrate, we need to know someone at a party. God can do anything." Within minutes, we approached a party where I knew a person well.

Case Study #3:

I desired for it to stop raining to do street evangelism. I went on a bus in the late evening believing it could possibly be not raining in East Lansing. I inquired on the bus, "Wouldn't it be amazing if it didn't rain in East Lansing?"

By the time we got to East Lansing, there was no rain.

Concept:

James 1:5 says, "If any of you lacks wisdom, let Him ask of God who gives generously without finding fault, but he must not doubt."

These case studies involved making requests known verbally by faith.

What do you want out of life?

My Story:

I am a Super Hero—sometimes misunderstood. In my opinion, if I do not shoot for the moon, what's the purpose?

God can do great things in us, but we must not settle for mediocrity.

Conclusion:

We need to ask God by faith for not just what we need, but what we desire.

Then, "Anticipate great things (Brian L. Arnold)."

Ever-Changing:

A Super Hero Manual Book

Chapter 10: Wise Words

Now that we have "freedom" and "confidence" as we approach God, we definitely should let go of unproductive dialogue.

As we approach our fellow man with love and forgiveness, let us be purposeful.

Paul in Ephesians 5, speaks of "always being thankful."

Thanksgiving should come out of our lips, instead of idle words.

Imagine the beauty of a person who shows discernment with his/her lips. If humankind uttered no idle words, wise men would tune in to every last word. To the least of these, we can be like a fresh fountain pouring out insight from the God within us. Shall we mix fresh spring water with a little bit of poisoned drink?

By all means no!

Let us be rather "making the most of every opportunity for the days are evil (Ephesians 5:16)." Let us be taken seriously by even the enemy as well as the allies.

"Submit yourselves therefore to God. Resist the devil, and he will flee from you (James 4:7)." "Clap your hands, all you nations; shout to God with cries of joy (Psalm 47:1)."

Ever-Changing:

A Super Hero Manual Book

Chapter 11: Pride

Puffed up, self-centered, egocentric.

Fictitious Case Study:

Johnny was completely focused on himself. He believed has was "the stuff."

He had a topnotch job, topnotch car and a topnotch girlfriend. He always believed that he could beat the system when he rebelled.

Unfortunately, for his ego, the IRS caught up with him. Due to his pride, he received the maximum sentence.

"Pride goes before destruction, a haughty spirit before a fall (Proverbs 16:18)." Super Heroes may have a heightened level of pride while in a state of mania.

This does not mean they should stop functioning. It does mean that they should keep pride in check. We all have wild thoughts. It is of value to control the tongue and let no idle words come out.

It is not bad to be confident, have a great car and a great significant other. However, pride must be eliminated in to prevent disaster.

The best place to start is giving glory to God instead of self.

The next step is to think of ourselves with "sober judgment" remembering that only Christ is perfect—knowing that everyone has weaknesses they are susceptible to.

Finally, give thanks again and recognize that it is only because of Jesus's sacrifice that we have any standing on earth or heaven.

<u>Ever-Changing:</u>

<u>A Super Hero Manual Book</u>

Chapter 12: Down Days

When you don't want to lift a finger and the world is moving faster than you, just pray. Some days it's difficult to get inspired. Some days I just want to sleep. On these days, just about everyone meshes with me the wrong way.

It's a down day—a great way to develop empathy.

Can breakthrough happen on a "down day?" My friend, that would be a breakthrough!

"For we walk by faith, not by sight (2 Corinthians 5:7)."

It may feel difficult to pull breakthrough out of a "down day," "but with God all things are possible (Matthew 19:26)."

The Lord God will "never leave" me "nor forsake" me. I find my rest in the Lord Almighty. I need His comfort, His Voice in my life. I rest in Him and I am safe.

Even at this moment, I am no longer down. I go through fluctuations. But through it all, God is with me. When I feel idle, I need to ask, Lord what do you want me to do?

What's on your heart Creator?

Keep going. Keep running that race. Everyone has "down days."

<u>Ever-Changing:</u>

<u>A Super Hero Manual Book</u>

Chapter 13: Philosophical Sanity

Is a break from sanity a holiness divergence? I want to be real, but it seems enjoyable to play the game of relapse.

What is right? What is wrong? Is it in the eye of the Beholder? Are there absolutes?

Am I writing this book?

Does God exist?

Philosophy is what it wants to be— including a break from sanity.

Unraveling the details and rearranging them—as if we were gods. If we are, who holds the stars in the sky?

Humans are born with inherent fallibilities.

We have found a way to get to the Moon, but the Universe?

I think not.

Humans have a habit of declaring absolute knowledge about what they haven't experienced.

If it's on the History Channel, it must be true.

Explain to me why God isn't real, when He speaks to me every day.

Should I be committed to a hospital for hearing the Voice of Truth?

One day, that may be a reality. The consequences of a belief system may result in sending a Christ-follower to eternity to dwell with Him.

To some, that is more of a reward than a punishment.

The Bible says, "For God did not give us a spirit of fear, but of power, of love, and of a sound mind (2 Timothy 1:7)."

Perhaps, it is definite that veering from sanity deliberately is sin itself.

What if the purpose you are acting— is to play a part in stage production that builds awareness?

It seems that there is a place for deliberate breeches of sanity, but in the real world typically not.

How a person behaves is between him/her and God. This is the same God I talk to on a daily basis.

I just want to be real. I need to stop putting on a show. If I'm going to be a "fool," let it be for Christ. My Judge is the Lord!

Ever-Changing:

A Super Hero Manual Book

Chapter 14: In The Sun

Definition:

Spotlight, Focus, Star-Struck, Focal Point, In The Limelight

Key Verse:

"Humble yourselves in the sight of the Lord and He shall lift you up (James 4:10)."

Our focus needs to be on Christ. Christ was focused on glorifying the Father. We are to model after Him.

Christ set an example and lived a perfect life. He is God incarnate. No man/woman should put the focus on another man/woman or Super Hero for humankind is fallible.

Thank you Jesus for your patience with me. So often I focus on myself--

trying to be a Super Star for my own glory.

Not even Jesus tried to be the Super Star. He gave all glory unto God. A Super Star falls unless that Super Star is the Godhead.

Even though a member of the Godhead, Christ, was a Super Star, He took the nature of a servant and became obedient to death on a cross. (Philippians 2)

If a person takes a leadership role in this world, they should do it in humility. This is labeled "servant leadership." A servant leader concentrates on serving those he/she leads over and submitting to the leading of the Holy Spirit.

Question:
What do you think the Lord might be leading you to do today?

<u>Ever-Changing:</u>

<u>A Super Hero Manual Book</u>

Chapter 15: Neighbor's House

Key Verse: "Love your neighbor as yourself (Mark 12:31)."

You may be placed in a culture that is different from you. This is a gift from God. Differences make up diversity. Differences can be acclimated to. Differences should not be assumed to be evil on account of difference.

When at your neighbor's house, play by your neighbor's cultural rules—even if they are different from your own.

For instance, it is proper in many houses to take off your shoes.

Apostle Paul, faced cultural cues when he wrote a large part of the New Testament. His cultural standards applied to the Corinthian Church in that cultural time period.

We are to respect the cultural standards of different people's groups without assuming they are religious standards.

For instance, in Arabic countries, it seems to be the tradition to display religious texts on high places. The bathroom or floor is considered disrespectful.

We need to make an effort to "be all things to all people as to win some" for Christ.

Why lose an audience over traditional matters?

Respect the culture of others.

Ever-Changing:

A Super Hero Manual Book

Chapter 16: Alive and Well

It is discourteous to negatively judge the mood of a Super Hero. As moods can fluctuate from moment to moment, encouragement works best.

Misery does not always love company.

In fact, the worst action you can take can be saying to a miserable creature: "You look depressed today."

Stay away from that label. On the same token, do not tell a jolly soul, "You seem manic."

Let a man enjoy his pleasing feeling. If he says something out of line, correct what he said—not the happy mood!

For many excuses exist to be non-functioning. I have written many chapters in a so-called altered state. If I was constantly waiting to be in an ideal mood—nothing would get done!

Give people grace. They serve God and do not bow down to you.

Let happy people be jolly. Let normal people praise God. Let sad people be encouraged.

Let everyone give thanks for being "alive and well."

Ever-Changing:

A Super Hero Manual Book

Chapter 17: Flesh

Word Association:

Being human, frail, of the world, sinful nature.

Is the flesh psychotic? It very well might be. For it brings death. It cannot please God.

 In this culture, people use their illness(es) to explain their behaviors.

Yet, we are not of this world. We are to be set apart and live differently.

Can someone diagnosed Schizoaffective honor God?

"With God all things are possible (Mark 10:27)."

Yes, we are given a sound mind to claim. But are we to judge someone because they received a diagnosis from man—absolutely not!

Mister Energy Plus needs to determine to honor God whether up or down. He is proud of the uniqueness afforded to Him by God.

If he's not ashamed,
If he's obeying God,

Who are you to rain on his parade?

Thanks be to God.

"Let everything that has breath praise the Lord (Psalm 150:6)."

Ever-Changing:

A Super Hero Manual Book

Chapter 18: New Breakthrough

"His mercies begin afresh each morning. ... they are new every morning (Lamentations 3:23);" We must not forget, in the hour of New Breakthrough, that God is building the house. Everything we have is from Him. When we wake up in the morning, it's mercy. When we are forgiven each and every time, His mercy extends to us.

Sometimes I feel unworthy of that mercy, but feel I have to have good recovery time.

When I break God's policies, I should seek to have God fix the relationship ASAP.   I want to have communication with God.

This is only possible with "mercies" that "are new every morning."

I am thankful that God is always faithful to me, unlike myself. His perfection and consistency holds me together.

Praise the Lord.

<u>Ever-Changing:</u>

<u>A Super Hero Manual Book</u>

Chapter 19: Blah…

When motivation is not there, what's the best action to take? People expect us to have the inspiration. God is in us after all.

In these situations, we have to dig deeper. We have to climb into the depths of our soul, where the Holy Spirit dwells.

It's time to get alone with Our Maker.

"But the Comforter, which is the Holy Ghost, whom the Father will send in my name. He will teach you all things and bring all things to your remembrance (John 14:26)."

God help us because really who else can? Some have fought the same fight before, but there is an hour where everyone else is busy or asleep.

Jesus experienced this moment in the Garden of Gethsemane. We are surrounded by such a great cloud of witnesses. We cannot give up the fight!

We must plough ahead when we do not feel like it and build our spiritual/emotional muscles.

"With my God I can scale any wall (Psalm 18:29)."

On my own, I rot on earth and in Hell.

I need Jesus to function, literally.

When, "I am weak, He is strong (Jesus Loves Me This I Know)."

Thank you Lord!

Ever-Changing:

A Super Hero Manual Book

Chapter 20: Impulse

My first thought is not always the best. Stopping to pray is wisdom. Carnality has a tendency to come out with impulse.

Super Heroes veer on the side of impulsive tendencies when their diagnoses fall in the manic spectrum.

I would venture to hypothesize, having had swings of depression, any mental condition polar of normal can bring impulsive tendencies.

The best way to cope is with love. Surround yourself in the love of God and with people who love God. Go to God first, for people can let you down. God will, "never leave" us "nor forsake" us.

Serving God is real and is the best default decision. Consider your words and daily actions carefully. People are watching closely.

Some are sizing up whether they believe Christianity is real. Some are taking us to be hypocritical.

Some are seeing the Light of God in us.

Do not be guilt-ridden over the past impulsive mistakes. They can be forgiven and then washed away as white as snow. No memory is left of them—in God's mind. Do not be held down by others' bitterness. Move on and be blessed.

<u>Ever-Changing:</u>

<u>A Super Hero Manual Book</u>

Chapter 21: Smorgasbord

Heaven is not the only place that "my soul shall be delighted as with the richest of foods." Life on earth is a blessing for those who sit at God's table.

"You prepare a table in the presence of my enemies. You anoint my head with oil (Psalm 23:5)."

The blessed anointing is strong true believers who know the Spirit. They walk forward and blessings flow. "For we walk by faith, not by sight (2 Corinthians 5:7)."

It is a smorgasbord of spiritual food.

"For the kingdom of God is not a matter of eating and drinking, but of righteousness, peace and joy in the Holy Spirit (Romans 14:7)."

We are to be filled in such a way that does not end in a tummy ache. Instead, we are supposed to overfill like a fresh spring—sharing the precipitation of God's love with everyone.

"You prepare a table for me in the presence of my enemies. You anoint my head with oil. My cup overflows (Psalm 23:5,6)."

This overflowing love flows with a presence that knows **God is real**.

This is the blessing for true believers.

Getting filled with the Holy Ghost is not a magic occurrence but rather the reality of a satisfied soul that must share because he/she is bursting at the seams with joy.

Enter into the joy of the Lord. Open your Bible and ask God how.

"All things are possible with God (Mark 10:27)."

"Surely goodness and mercy shall follow me all the days of my life and I shall dwell in the house of the Lord forever (Psalm 23:6)."

Ever-Changing:

A Super Hero Manual Book

Chapter 22: Help

After the shock is over, no one wants to be "The Boy Who Cried Wolf."

There are ramifications to sounding the alarm. Consequences exist in this life for playing the attention-getter.

Yet, what if these emergencies are real and constant? What if we lived in a body in torment?

Would people cease to care about us? Would we become frustrated to the point of sounding the alarm?

Suffering is real and we must not be insensitive to those in chronic pain. I know of a young man who goes to the hospital frequently for different reasons.

His faith journey must be slightly different than mine and I do not know how to encourage him in his frustrating pain. What should I say? What should I do?

I will just be there for him.

A person suffering from chronic emergencies appreciates someone being there with him/her.

It can be lonely to suffer in isolation. I have family. I cannot imagine if I did not.

Perhaps, we are this person's family.

Be sensitive to those who suffer from chronic pain. Listen as best you can.

You may be entertaining an angel unaware.

<u>Ever-Changing:</u>

<u>A Super Hero Manual Book</u>

Chapter 23: Leisure

What a person does for leisure pertains to what he/she values.

Are we just "passing the time" or are we intentional about how we spend our "free time?"

Some are very busy, yet can pencil others in. Some have constant free time and still do not make time for others.

It seems there is always time for our priorities.

What are our priorities and do we consciously implement them into all aspects of life?

It is a mistake to fixate on priorities we cannot control. However, if we do not keep priorities in mind on some level, we may lose sight of them.

Obituaries are not what many people
want to think about from day to day.
Yet, legacy does become a priority
when time grows short.

What is important at the beginning
typically changes by the end of one's
life.

The rare people do not live last
minute fix-it-up lives, rather
consistent lives over time.

Daily they build into their legacy
piggy-bank, treasures in Heaven.

I think of one of them. He just passed
away into Glory Land.

His name is Charles Leverich. He
had poems to share and let his
generosity speak through his finances
to the audience of one—God.

I imagine that this man's spare time,
his leisure, was investing in others.

He will never be forgotten.

I want what I do to make a lasting impression on God' face. Right now, I am not selfless enough.

I let my mood be effected by circumstances from time to time. Still I know Jesus is Lord and I want to live for Him!

Super Heroes can be marginalized, but God knows their true legacy.

He is the final audience. As Paul said, "To live is Christ; to die is gain (Philippians 1:21)."

Let us live and prioritize our lives with eternal perspective.

Ever-Changing:

A Super Hero Manual Book

Chapter 24: Love

If you read 1 John quickly, you may summarize that to continue sinning is not to know God.

Looking, closely, there is a provision made for repentance.

1 John 1:9 "If we confess our sins, He is faithful and just to forgive our sins and to cleanse us from all unrighteousness."

Love is what it's all about. Love for God and fellow man is the summary of the Scripture – especially love for enemies.

It is time to take a stand for righteousness and care for those in need.

It is time to be set apart and have that saltiness that makes Christians different—being uniquely salty.

People are hurting and when we are in sin, our spirits are hurting.

Love is what's needed to change the world—not the condemnation of the devil.

Shall we hold back the truth because it offends?

God forbid. Walk the right path and testify to the goodness of God!

If we as believers do not speak up, who will bring the good news? "Beautiful are the feet of them which bring good news (Romans 10:15)!"

Ever-Changing:

A Super Hero Manual Book

Chapter 25: Take Me Home

There will be a day, when all pain is gone. We will have new bodies. "But as it is written, Eye hath not seen, nor ear heard, neither have entered into the heart of man, the things which God hath prepared for them that love him (1 Corinthians 2:9)." I've never seen Heaven, but it will be better than anything I could ever imagine. Surely, it will be deep Communion with the Everlasting God.

No more curses. No more pain. No more light needed; for the glory of the Lord will shine. One focus, One God, One Accord. We will come together to praise the Lord.

It will be our passion to do this as it should be now. Let's "run in such a way as to get the prize (1 Corinthians

9:24)." Let's put Christ first in this life and the lay down our crowns in the next.

For God is worthy of all adoration.

Ever-Changing:

A Super Hero Manual Book

Chapter 26: Encouragement

There are moments when Super Heroes fall on the floor, down for the count, ready to tap out.

It is at these moments, "…We walk by faith, not by sight (2 Corinthians 5:7)." God is real and He will come through for His children in unexpected ways.

Where does my hope from when everyone has fled the scene? God is my hope and "God works in mysterious ways."

Mysterious: The despised people looked down upon can be there for you in your time of need.

"But God chose the foolish things of the world to shame the wise (1 Corinthians 1:27);"

Today, a street minister cared about me when I left the building where ministry was taking place.

I did not know she and her team cared so much. They prayed over me immediately. They stopped the order of the meeting for me—one soul.

This is how God's heart operates.

There is more joy in Heaven when one sinner repents than over a fold of 100 righteous.

You can lightly sprinkle a congregation of a hundred or can drench one desperate parched soul on the brink of disaster.

Thank you Jesus for sending a seemingly invisible ministry to reach the invisible.

Use their work to change the world— one city at a time.

Conclusion:

Encouragement becomes epic when it considers every last soul.

Ever-Changing:

A Super Hero Manual Book

Chapter 27: Sticking With It

The Bible says, "We will reap a harvest if we don't give up (Galatians 6:9)." Investing in people is a huge, meaningful, endeavor.

When we pour into lives, we pour into souls. We must have substance ourselves, something to give, but every deposit counts.

Do not give up on people. See hope in every life, every opportunity. Stand your ground for the Lord as a good soldier. Love always. Never quit loving.

Never give up on a person this side of Heaven. The Lord knows the heart. We are meant to see hope.

"For I know the plans I have for you," declares the LORD, "plans to prosper you and not to harm you, plans to give you hope and a future (Jeremiah 29:11)."   Never let up. If you give up on a person or a person's vision, you may injure that person's motivation.

See the hope in every soul and give your best to investing in others.

It will reap eternal dividends.

Morale:

Take eyes off self and love others to the end as Christ loved and gave Himself for us.

<u>Ever-Changing:</u>

<u>A Super Hero Manual Book</u>

Chapter 28: Deletion

Defined:

Removal, Microsoft Trash, To Take Away, Eliminate.

No more. No More. Many times, it seems, life has friends that shouldn't be around. Full-throttle, for whatever reason, the Super Hero may believe he/she needs to go on a deleting spree.

Overkill, is overkill. Hopefully, no bridges have been burned.

When a Super Hero does not know what to do, he/she might hit the delete button. Bye-Bye career, Bye-Bye Church and the friends that goes with it!

The secret to happiness is not always CTRL-ALT-DELETE. Sometimes there is a backdoor.

However, everyone needs a vacation once in awhile. Basically, no one has it all together all the time. Give Super Heroes a little breathing room so we can breathe. You will be thankful you did.

Ever-Changing:

A Super Hero Manual Book

Chapter 29: Reality

I want to write something incredible, weighty, substantial, and real.

My reality is Jesus Christ. I do not claim to understand every perplexity, preponderance, or supposed contradiction.

All I claim is that He is in me and for me. All I can testify is that He has improved my life and the life of others.

Does the History Channel dispute God? Not anymore than the original Adversary, challenging liar did when he put himself out of paradise.

Dynasties will rise and dynasties will fall. The truth of God remains applicable to my life.

I may not always apply it. I may not always live by it, but I walk by the faith that reveals itself with time.

We all need a Comforter, a God who communicates with us.

We may not always hear clearly, but the music is playing.

"For we walk by faith not by sight (2 Corinthians 5:7)."

<u>Ever-Changing:</u>

<u>A Super Hero Manual Book</u>

Chapter 30: Where (Many) Super Heroes Worship

When there is no place to go, this is where people go. City Outreach, aka Bozzo's is a place of mercy, for many of Lansing's broken on Sunday Morning.

There is food, love, mercy, rough edges meeting rough edges. I think of Jesus reaching the 12 disciples with raw love, boldness.

Not everyone is smiling, in fact many are screaming inside. Some haven't had a good night sleep in the changing Michigan weather in months.

This is the place where love shines down through food, a rebuke, an effortful smile.

Jesus said, "The King will reply, 'Truly I tell you, whatever you did for one of the least of these brothers and sisters of mine, you did for me (Matthew 25:40)." This is Lansing's hotspot of "faith, hope, and love."

<u>Ever-Changing:</u>

<u>A Super Hero Manual Book</u>

Chapter 31: Waiting

Breakthrough does not happen overnight always. Breakthrough usually takes a tremendous amount of mental effort called faith.

Hold it together. Do not give up. Push forward by faith.

With man it may be impossible. "But with God all things are possible (Matthew 19:26)."

Never let up on living. Never let up on waiting for God's promises to come to pass. You may be waiting for provision, a career, the right spouse to come into your life.

In your time of waiting, obey God, serve God, be thankful! Read the Bible and stand on it.

"Faith is the substance of things hoped for, the evidence of things unseen (Hebrews 11:1)." Take the time to not just wait for your own miracle, but be the God-send miracle in another's life!

Love "always hopes, trusts, perseveres (1 Corinthians 13:7)." Persevere in being a good, giving, loving soldier and know that your blessing is coming.

"Delight thyself also in the LORD; and he shall give thee the desires of thine heart (Psalm 37:4)."

What do you desire most?

What is important to you?

When we bless others while waiting, our world can turn right side up!

Live your dreams.

If you aren't paid, see your dreams come to pass pro bono.

Watch God take care of you! His love is unending.

Serving the broken is serving Him.

Theme:

Do the work of the Lord as you wait to see your dreams come to pass by faith.

Ever-Changing:

A Super Hero Manual Book

Chapter 32: Conclusion

Life is an ever-changing world. Today is not the same as yesterday. "Tomorrow is not promised." The present is not to be worried about and can change.

You have read these pages about the life of a Super Hero. Where the saga begins is of little importance compared to the journey and destination.

Share the journey. Run the race. Do not give up.

Thanks,

Daniel K. Arnold